CHOOSING A
Life
THAT MATTERS

Books by Dennis and Barbara Rainey

*Barbara and Susan's Guide
to the Empty Nest* (with Susan Yates)*

*Letters to My Daughters**

Moments with You: Daily Connections for Couples

Moments Together for Couples

Moments Together for Growing Closer to God

Moments Together for Intimacy

Moments Together for Living What You Believe

Moments Together for Parents

Moments Together for a Peaceful Home

*Preparing for Marriage***

*Preparing for Marriage Leader's Guide***

Preparing for Marriage Devotions for Couples

So You Want to Be a Teenager

Books by Dennis Rainey

Stepping Up

Interviewing Your Daughter's Date

Aggressive Girls, Clueless Boys

* Barbara Rainey
** Dennis Rainey, General Editor

CHOOSING A
Life
THAT MATTERS

7 Decisions
You'll Never Regret

DENNIS RAINEY

WITH

TIM GRISSOM

BETHANYHOUSE
a division of Baker Publishing Group
Minneapolis, Minnesota

© 2017 by Dennis Rainey

Published by Bethany House Publishers
11400 Hampshire Avenue South
Bloomington, Minnesota 55438
www.bethanyhouse.com

Bethany House Publishers is a division of
Baker Publishing Group, Grand Rapids, Michigan

Printed in the United States of America

Library of Congress Control Number: 2017945475

ISBN 978-0-7642-1973-3

Scripture quotations, unless otherwise noted, are from The Holy
Bible, English Standard Version® (ESV®), copyright © 2001 by
Crossway, a publishing ministry of Good News Publishers. Used
by permission. All rights reserved. ESV Text Edition: 2011

Scripture quotations marked NASB are from the New American Standard Bible®, copyright © 1960, 1962, 1963, 1968, 1971, 1972, 1973,
1975, 1977, 1995 by The Lockman Foundation. Used by permission.
(www.Lockman.org)

Emphasis in Scripture, shown by italics, is the author's.

Unattributed poems are the author's.

Cover design by Dan Thornberg, Design Source Creative Services.

Author is represented by Wolgemuth & Associates.

17   18   19   20   21   22   23   7   6   5   4   3   2

To Josh Dries
To whom I gave my last daughter,
Laura Victoria,
On October 22, 2016
You are The Man!

Contents

Introduction

The Journey

I have lived almost seven decades. Most of these years have been adventurous—packed with new vistas, familiar paths, mysteries, messes, mountaintops, and a few dark valleys. All have resulted in discoveries about God, life, self, and people. One of the most important discoveries came from reading A.W. Tozer's *The Knowledge of the Holy* and being challenged with his statement: "What comes into our minds when we think about God is the most important thing about us."

I want to tell you two stories that explain why I've not been able to get away from that statement for almost half a century.

An Unlikely Messenger

About a decade ago, I received a call from the president
of Trinity International University and Trinity Evan-
gelical Divinity School informing me that they wanted
to confer an honorary doctorate on me for three decades of work on behalf of marriages and families.
He then invited me to speak at their commencement
ceremonies.

I was humbled to receive such an honor and sur-
prised that they would ask me to address the gradu-
ating classes of both the university and the seminary.
Although I had a graduate degree from Dallas Theological Seminary, I didn't have a doctorate. I could picture myself standing in front of hundreds of professors,
most of them with PhDs from prestigious institutions,
and reading their thoughts: "What's a guy like him
doing in a place like this?"

Even so, I accepted the invitation. Then a second
emotion took over: fear. What could I say to the under-
grads and seminarians that would be of any value?
They'd studied under some of the top biblical scholars
in the world. Hadn't they pretty much heard it all?
And so I did what I try to do whenever I'm confronted
with an opportunity that taps into my inadequacies: I
prayed. For months.

As I prayed I began to think about these students and what they were going to do. Many would go to work for corporations, some would become pastors, others would be teachers, professors, authors, and some would pioneer ministries both domestic and global. Others would take jobs in every imaginable sector of our economy. A few would serve in the military.

Each one would be stepping out of the spiritual incubator of the classroom and into the rushing stream of God's work. They'd experience life—the challenges and benefits of marriage, children, bills, debt, health issues, and the like—all while attempting to walk with God and faithfully obey Him. Real family life.

A question began to form in my mind: Could I give them, in one message, the essence of what the Bible teaches about what God expects of us? I wasn't under any delusion that a single message would change their world, but I was determined to prepare something that would contribute to their lives beyond graduation day, something that would help them to choose a life that matters.

As I prayerfully reflected on the major themes of Scripture where I'd experienced God repeatedly in my life, I began crafting life lessons regarding how we are to think about Him, what He expects of us, and how we should relate to Him. I wanted to give them a taste of the marrow of the Christian life. These lessons were shaved and culled, and eventually took the form of seven "essence statements."

In reviewing "The 7," I then began to notice that each of these positive commands of Scripture was contrasted with warnings and countering commands. Every "Do this" had a corresponding "Don't do that."

Now, I know that walking with God and experiencing the reality of Him cannot be reduced to a list of do's and don'ts. However, these clear commands of Scripture have served me well as boundaries and have directed my thoughts to God and living for His glory and pleasure. It is in that spirit that I offer them to you in this book.

You might ask, "Are they really 'THE 7'?" It would be arrogant to claim that I've found "THE 7." My challenge to you is to take a look at these and see if you can find a better seven, or reduce them to two, as Jesus did when He was asked, "What is the greatest commandment?" There may be twelve. Send me your pass at it after you've tested it for a decade. But anchor them in the Scriptures.

Which brings me to the second story I promised you.

Box Tops and Puzzles

Over the period of nearly a dozen years, I had the high privilege of teaching a sixth grade Sunday school class, totaling more than 550 young men and women. To illustrate our need of the Scriptures, I would divide the classes into three groups of twenty to twenty-five each (they were big classes). I would give each of the three groups a jigsaw puzzle. One group would receive a 1,000-piece puzzle in its original box. Another group would receive a 1,000-piece puzzle, but not in the correct box. Finally, the third group would receive a 1,000-piece puzzle in a paper bag. I would then instruct them not to talk and that they had seven minutes to put as much of their puzzle together as possible.

Every time, the first group would stand up their box top, which displayed what the puzzle should look like, and begin making progress. The second group would look at the box top and attempt to put their puzzle together. After a couple of minutes, they would tell me they'd been tricked and that it wasn't fair. The third group would empty their pieces from the bag and immediately know that they were at a huge disadvantage. After just a few minutes of trying to assemble a few pieces, their despair would take over and they'd begin tossing puzzle pieces at one another like miniature Frisbees.

After the time was up, I'd gather the class together and explain what they all knew; the right box top was necessary to put the puzzle together. I then shared with them that God knew we'd need a "picture" of who He is, what He is like, and how we as finite creatures can relate to Him, the infinite Creator. This was why God gave us the Scriptures. The Bible is God's box top that explains Him and life as He designed it to be lived.

I went on to explain that since creation, humankind has been ignoring God's box top and has been trying on its own to piece life together. But it never turns out as God intends.

This is what I tried to communicate in my commencement address to those university and seminary students. The Bible not only explains who God is, His attributes and character, but it also clearly explains who we are and how God expects us to relate to Him.

* ◌ * ◌ * ◌ *

The longer I live the more strongly I agree with Mr. Tozer: What we think about God really is the most important thing. And it's not just that other things will matter less in comparison; it's that other things won't matter at all. If we get this one thing wrong or, worse yet, neglect it entirely, life will be essentially meaningless. So if you want a life that matters, your quest for knowing God matters—more than anything else.

God is not some kind of cosmic killjoy, hiding from us. As you'll read in the pages that follow, He wants us to seek Him, to find Him, know Him, and love Him. He puts himself in our path regularly. Many of the events that we call interruptions, many of the circumstances that we call setbacks, and many of the people that we call difficult are, in reality, God's agents to introduce us to Him. He has strategically positioned them to help us realize how deeply we need Him, to prove over and over again that all our deficiencies are canceled out by His grace and that all our needs are met in Him.

Oh, what a Savior!

So do not expect to find in these pages a menu of solutions that can be matched against your problems. This will read more like a guidebook for tourists, offering advice for the journey: how to prepare, what places to avoid, and where to go for help and refreshment.

May God be honored in your journey.

—Dennis Rainey
November 2016

1

Seek God, Not Sin

For thus says the LORD to the house of Israel:
"Seek me and live."

—Amos 5:4

Several years ago, when we first started our *Weekend
to Remember* marriage getaways, I was speaking in
Kansas City. Because our ministry budget did not yet
allow for spouses to travel along, Barbara was not with
me. After a full day of speaking, I grabbed a quick dinner and went up to my hotel room to relax. Kicking off
my shoes and stretching out on the bed, I called home
to check in. Barbara and I talked for several minutes,
and after hanging up I turned on a movie. When the

phone rang, I thought perhaps Barbara had forgotten to tell me something. Instead, on the other end of the line was a woman I didn't know. Our brief conversation went like this:

ME: Hello.

HER: Hey! What are you doing?

ME: I'm watching a movie.

HER: Can I come up?

ME: I don't think that would be a good idea.

HER: I'd really like to come up. Why wouldn't that be a good idea?

ME: For two reasons. First, I'm married to this great lady back in Little Rock, and we've pledged a covenant of love together with God that neither of us will break. And second, the movie I'm watching is *The Ten Commandments*!

With that, I hung up.

You and I Are Being Stalked

Whenever I think of that incident, I'm reminded of what God said to Cain: "If you do well, will you not be accepted? And if you do not do well, *sin is crouching at the door. Its desire is for you, but you must rule over it*" (Genesis 4:7). I realized that in that moment I was being stalked, and not just by a wannabe adulteress. Sin itself was stalking me; it always is. Sin stays in attack mode, ready to pounce without warning.

Sin comes masked as a sultry woman looking to hook up with a man away from home, or in the polluted stream of pornography that is just one convenient click away on our web browser. Or through a "friendship" with a person of the opposite sex who is meeting emotional needs designed only for marriage. Or in daydreams of a better spouse—a different one. And sin takes more subtle forms—a stab of jealousy when we see a new car sitting in our neighbor's driveway, or the resentment we pile up against our spouse each time he or she disappoints us. Sin is as nearby as our hands, eyes, ears, feet, or heart—any of the temptation gateways Satan likes to use to divert us from knowing God.

Sadly, when I told that story at another marriage conference, a woman in attendance called my room later in the evening and asked to come up. This time there was no conversation, I just hung up. The next day a woman came up and confessed that she was the one who'd called and that her husband, who was standing there with her, had put her up to calling me. She said, "He wanted to see if you really are in private who you claim to be in public!"

You Were Made for This

Our hearts were made to hunger, which is one reason temptation can pull us so easily along. We come with a factory setting of dissatisfaction (which is different than discontentment, but I digress) that drives us beyond the status quo. We don't want life to always be as it has always been. We want to grow, learn, add, change, and conquer. And while it is true that this drive can take us down paths of selfishness, arrogance, and sin, it doesn't have to go that way. We can—and should—"hunger and thirst for righteousness" (Matthew 5:6). Our dissatisfaction can be sanctified, and it can lead us down paths of holiness and seeking God. As Christian men and women, we were made to want to know and experience more of God, to seek Him.

We find the idea of seeking God referenced more than fifty times in the Bible. Sometimes it came as a call to an individual, while at other times to a group, or even a nation. Sometimes it was a call to repent from evil and destructive behavior, while at other times it was a promise of increased blessing to those already walking with God—all of which underscores the truth that God's children need to be seeking Him. Always. Here are just a few examples; as you read these, notice how many have promises and what is promised.

And you, Solomon my son, know the God of your father and serve him with a whole heart and with a willing mind, for the LORD searches all hearts and understands every plan and thought. If you seek him, he will be found by you, but if you forsake him, he will cast you off forever.

1 Chronicles 28:9

The Spirit of God came upon Azariah the son of Oded, and he went out to meet Asa and said to him, "Hear me, Asa, and all Judah and Benjamin: The LORD is with you while you are with him. If you seek him, he will be found by you, but if you forsake him, he will forsake you."

2 Chronicles 15:1–2

The LORD is near to all who call on him, to all who call on him in truth.

Psalm 145:18

Seek the LORD while he may be found; call upon him while he is near.

Isaiah 55:6

You will seek me and find me, when you seek me with all your heart.

Jeremiah 29:13

Seek the LORD and live.

Amos 5:6

Follow me, and I will make you fishers of men.

Matthew 4:19

Draw near to God, and he will draw near to you. . . . Humble yourselves before the Lord, and he will exalt you.

James 4:8, 10

A cursory reading of these and other Scriptures leads me to two conclusions:

1. God wants us to seek Him.
2. Our hearts were made to seek Him.

God wants us to seek Him. Why? Is He toying with us, resetting the goal each time we are just about to reach it? Is He being unfair?

Of course God isn't being unfair. Look again at the verses you just read and see the hope and promise in them: "He will be found by you"; "The LORD is near"; "He may [can] be found"; "You . . . will find me"; "Live"; "I will make you"; "He will draw near." Do these describe a God who is playing mind games with His children, or do they sound like the promises of the God who knows that all that is best for us can be found in Him, so He draws us into the search? God doesn't invite us to seek Him so He can hide, He invites us to seek Him so we will find Him!

Our hearts were made to seek Him. God has extended the invitation to seek Him to all of His children, but all do not RSVP. Here, in Psalm 27:8, we see one who did. David wrote, "You have said, 'Seek my face.' My heart says to you, 'Your face, LORD, do I seek.'"

This is David being true to his nature as a child of God. He is showing the same spiritual fortitude that Joshua did when he stood out among his faith-faltering countrymen:

> And if it is evil in your eyes to serve the LORD, choose this day whom you will serve, whether the gods your

fathers served in the region beyond the River, or the gods of the Amorites in whose land you dwell. But as for me and my house, we will serve the LORD.

Joshua 24:15

When we don't seek God, when we shift into neutral and choose either to glide along on our own past accomplishments or ride the coattails of others who are stronger, we are being untrue to our Christian identity. We are drifting. Atrophying. Weakening. Seeking God demands that we use our spiritual muscles in the lifelong quest of finding Him.

Failing to seek God is a setup for sin to seek us and rob us of our identity. Sin distracts us from our spiritual mission and purpose. Neglecting to seek God marks the onset of spiritual anemia. Soul fatigue generally comes from doing too little rather than too much.

There is a remedy. Seek God!

LIFE SKILL: How to seek God

Wisdom is godly skill for everyday living. It is the application of knowledge (the truth as found in Scripture) in how to "do life" the way God designed it. Wisdom takes the raw components of life and skillfully crafts them, makes them beautiful and purposeful as God intended life to be.

Why am I telling you this? Because when I read a book or blog that inspires me to make a change but doesn't give me any guidance for implementing that change, I feel let down. I've only received half of what I need. For that reason, I'm including a Life Skill section in each chapter. I want you to do more than think about what you read on these pages; I want you to actually do something with it. I want to help you grow in wisdom.

When I came to the conclusion that I needed to be more intentional about seeking God, I soon faced the very practical question of how? Did this mean that I should read more books? Listen to more sermons? Move to a monastery? I wasn't sure what I needed to do.

Now, I admit that I'm an activity junkie. I thrive on motion and exertion. Even my leisure activities are, well, active. Sitting still doesn't come naturally to me. So if seeking God meant isolation and becoming sedentary, I didn't see the appeal.

I hope you didn't miss what I said, that I needed to be more *intentional* about seeking God, because to me, that is a key point. Seeking God requires a determination, a commitment, a wholehearted pursuit. We won't wish our way into it; there's no such thing as an ambivalent God seeker. The apostle Paul sure didn't think so. Listen as he describes his own approach to seeking God:

> Indeed, I count everything as loss because of the surpassing worth of knowing Christ Jesus my Lord. For his sake I have suffered the loss of all things and count them as rubbish, in order that I may gain Christ and be found in him, not having a righteousness of my own that comes from the law, but that which comes through faith in Christ, the righteousness from God that depends on faith—that I may know him and the power of his resurrection, and may share his sufferings, becoming like him in his death, that by any means possible I may attain the resurrection from the dead. Not that I have already obtained this or am already perfect, but I press on to make it my own, because Christ Jesus has made me his own.
>
> Philippians 3:8–12

There wasn't anything halfhearted in the way Paul pursued God, was there? "I count everything as loss . . . I have suffered the loss of all things . . . I press on." Why did he do it? "Because of the surpassing worth of knowing Christ . . . that I may know him . . . becoming like him." Wow! That's what I want too—to be like Christ. But it won't come easy and I won't get there from my recliner.

Where Is God?

If God is present everywhere, and He is, then there is no place where we cannot find Him. But we must look. We must continually seek Him.

He is present in creation. When is the last time you marveled at the Creator's ingenuity? Go take a walk and ask God to help you find Him.

His character and ways are found in the Scriptures. Instead of just reading the Bible, search its pages and ask Him to help you find Him. You will find the most accurate description of God there.

He is present in His people—His image bearers. When's the last time you related to another person as a carrier of His image, imprinted with God's DNA?

You can learn more about Him through music and other forms of art.

You can learn more about Him through reading biographies of those who spent a lifetime seeking Him.

You can seek God in solitude. Read the Bible, and then be still and listen.

You can seek God in worship with fellow believers.

You can seek God through prayer.

You will find God if you keep looking.

And Thus I Pondered

I came to realize, however, that along with my intentionality—which fed my active nature—I needed something more for my approach to seeking God. Through the Old Testament book of Ecclesiastes, I learned that I needed to become a ponderer.

> In addition to being a wise man, the Preacher also taught the people knowledge; and he pondered, searched out and arranged many proverbs.
>
> Ecclesiastes 12:9 NASB

This spoke to me because, frankly, I hadn't done much true pondering. I was more of a reactive thinker, concentrating my thoughts mostly on what was going on at the moment. But here was this wise man, the Preacher, giving away one of the secrets to his wisdom—he pondered.

The Preacher (Solomon) is an example to us of one who was intentional about seeking God. He set his mind and heart to it (Ecclesiastes 1:13; 2:11–12). He was driven by the vanity he saw around him, and sometimes even within his own heart, to make sense of life from a heavenly perspective. He was not a fatalist, as some have accused; he simply used the dark side of life to reveal the light. But this would not have happened—he would not have grown in wisdom, and we could not have benefited from his insights—if he had not stopped, thought, and pondered life from God's vantage point.

This is what seeking God can do for you. So I ask: When have you—or have you ever—sought God with your whole heart?

A Beginner's Guide to Pondering

As I continued through my meditations of the book of Ecclesiastes, I developed this list. I share this with you not to promote the idea that seeking and knowing God can be accomplished through formulae. God is relational. However, this list serves as a tool for pondering the many ways God intersects my life and where I need His wisdom.

1. Prepare a time and place to pray through this list on my own.
   - Ponder: What is my world doing to me?
   - What am I doing to my world?
   - Where is God at work in my world?
   - How could I join Him in His work?
2. Reflect on:
   - My relationship with God—First grade through twelfth, what "grade" am I in right now in relationship with God? What must you do to graduate to the next grade?
   - God's purpose for my life—Can I summarize it?
   - My priorities and activities
   - What is God currently doing in my life?

- What is He wanting me to step out in faith and trust Him with?
- My values—what is He affirming? What is He convicting me of that I need to change?
- My direction (Where will I be ten years from today? What should I be doing now in order to get there?)
- My convictions
- My commitments
- The general state and trajectory of my life—be ruthlessly honest—where is it taking me?

3. Take inventory of the resources God has given me.
   - How does God want to use my personality?
   - What are my talents, and how does God want to use them?
   - How has God trained me, and what other training does He want me to pursue?
   - What are my spiritual gifts, and how does God want to use them?
   - What are my convictions? What has He uniquely gifted me to do?

4. Consider what God expects of me:
   - In my relationships
   - In my job
   - In my church
   - In my community

5. So what? Aspire to new territories: What is God giving me a vision, a passion, and a desire for? What would I do, what would I attempt, if I knew I could not fail?

2

···

Fear God, Not Men

The fear of the LORD leads to life, and whoever has it rests satisfied; he will not be visited by harm.

—Proverbs 19:23

It's a lesson I'll never forget.

Several years ago, my ten-year-old son Benjamin and I were clearing brush and trees along the west edge of our property. Our house sits on a wooded ridge, overlooking a lake. The view is magnificent, especially at sunset. In fact, our back deck is one of my favorite spots in the world; there I have a reserved seat for God's daily sky show over thirteen ridges of the Ouachita Mountains. It's a spiritual experience. Seriously.

The problem was that a few trees had begun to crowd my view, which explains why Benjamin and I were lumberjacking. We cut, pulled, piled, and sweated until we eventually came to the worst offender, a tall oak. It was a beautiful tree in its own right, but it was stealing my view and thus had to go.

At this point I should tell you that our west property line adjoins a forest that is owned by the city of Little Rock, and the offending oak straddled the line. As I fired up the chainsaw and was about to start cutting, Benjamin stopped me. "Isn't this tree on city property?" he asked.

"No," I shouted over the roar of the saw. "Not necessarily. Property lines are never that exact out here in the woods. Besides, there are millions of trees. They'll never miss this one."

Soon the oak came crashing down, the stump now providing evidence that it had actually been just over the line, on the city's property. I had a tinge of regret (or was it guilt?), but my enthusiasm for a new and improved view quickly muffled those feelings. But they returned the next morning when I stood on the deck and all I could see was that horizontal oak, a monument to my compromised integrity.

After a couple more days, I didn't even want to go out on the deck. I couldn't enjoy the view, and the guilt wouldn't go away. It seemed like every passage I read in the Bible included trees. Clearly, the Lord wasn't going to leave me alone about this. I finally faced the reality that I needed to call the city offices and confess my indiscretion and poor judgment.

I wish I could say that I obeyed right away, but instead I tried to talk God out of having me make the call. I delayed for two full months. But, as Thomas Carlyle once said, "Conviction, were it never so excellent, is worthless till it converts itself into conduct," and it was time for me to man up. I made the call in the presence of my son. (Since he saw me commit the crime, I thought it best if he witnessed me turning myself in.) As the call connected, I secretly wished for someone to answer that I didn't know. Instead, I found myself on the line with a city employee who lived nearby—practically one of our neighbors. I told him who I was and what I'd done: "I cut down a tree on city property, just across from my own. I was wrong to do that and I want to make restitution."

I expected to be threatened with prosecution, or maybe a hefty fine, but the man was very gracious. He thanked me for my call. And then he said, "The property lines out there aren't that exact anyway."

After the call was over, I looked my son Benjamin in the eyes—the son who'd now witnessed the crime, the confession, and now the reprieve—and said, "Son, what I did was wrong, and God didn't let me off the hook. You will not remember me as a perfect dad, but I do want you to remember me as a dad who attempted to walk with God and sought to please Him, that when I was wrong, I confessed it and did what was right."

A Hundred Lesser Evils

A.W. Tozer wrote, "The low view of God entertained almost universally among Christians is the cause of a hundred lesser evils everywhere among us."[1] The threshold for sin is lowered or raised in proportion to our view of God. My rationalizing cutting down a tree that didn't belong to me, and ignoring God's conviction about it for two months, exposed something about my heart that I didn't like. My view of God was too low.

When we lower our view of God, we lose our sense of being accountable to Him. This makes it easier to excuse all sorts of evil in our lives—from "little white lies" to infidelity, and all points in between. We sin more easily when we think less of God.

The habit of excusing sin is often set in motion by comparison. If we analyze our lives according to how other Christians live, we begin to justify our behavior based on the law of averages—what is going on in the larger Christian community. Rather than seeking to know and please God, we become content to fit comfortably within the Christian subculture. Again, Mr. Tozer causes us to reflect: "We have accepted one another's notions and copied one another's lives and made one another's experiences the model for our own."[2] To make matters worse, as the state of the general Christian community trends downward and becomes soft on sin, so do our lives. We are a people adrift who desperately need to reclaim that part of our belief system known as the fear of the Lord.

Fearing God

To fear God means to be in awe of Him, to revere Him. Yes, God is our friend, but we are certainly not His equal. God is above us in every way. He is holy, almighty, sovereign, righteous, and just. He "can destroy both soul and body in hell" (Matthew 10:28).

We don't hear much about the fear of God today and we seldom speak of the wrath and judgment of God. When these things are preached, one can't help but have a healthy sense of fear and awe, but we'd rather keep humanity's sin and God's wrath out of the discussion and circle up for a group hug around "a cushy god" that's little more than an oversized marshmallow. It's the more agreeable and manageable way.

Wilbur Rees exposes our malady:

> I'd like to buy $3 worth of God, please.
> Not enough to explode my soul or disturb
>   my sleep,
> But just enough to equal a cup of warm milk
> Or a snooze in the sunshine.
> I don't want enough of God to make me love
>   a black man
> Or pick beets with a migrant.
> I want ecstasy, not transformation.
> I want the warmth of the womb, not a new
>   birth.
> I want a pound of the Eternal in a paper
>   sack.
> I would like to buy $3 worth of God, please.[3]

In my study of the Scriptures and observations of life, I've concluded that fearing God generally displays itself in four ways:

1. Reverential awe of God's nature
2. Awareness of God's presence
3. Holy dread of displeasing God
4. Growing hatred of evil

As you read these brief descriptions, consider how they are—if they are—present in your life.

Reverential awe of God's nature

In his book *Man in the Mirror*, Patrick Morley observed this:

> Cultural Christianity means to pursue the God we want instead of the God who is. It is the tendency to be shallow in our understanding of God, wanting Him to be more of a gentle grandfather type who spoils us and lets us have our own way. It is sensing a need for God, but on our own terms. It is wanting the God we have underlined in our Bibles without wanting the rest of Him too. It is God relative rather than God absolute.[4]

Morley describes on a cultural level what is happening to many of us on a personal level: pursuing God as we want Him to be and not as He truly is. But God will have none of it.

Looking back on my early life as a boy, two things shaped my respect and fear for God. One was the church I grew up in. The preaching that came from the pulpit was vivid in its description of God's character, including His wrath and judgment of sin. The topic of hell was frequently addressed. Whenever the pastor peached about hell, it seemed like the pulpit tipped toward the congregation and smoldering brimstone poured down the aisle. It was scary to a little boy then, and it still is to a grown man now—and rightfully so. But that preaching was anchored in the redeeming love of God extended through Christ. I'm grateful for the emphasis of both the fear of God and the love of God.

I also learned to fear God from my dad. He was a man whose character was so solid that he commanded respect without ever uttering a word. He had so much integrity that I like to say the only thing that was wicked about my dad was his curve ball. Dad was not perfect, but he was an honorable man. All you needed was my dad's word and a handshake.

Awareness of God's presence

If you were to put in the time and effort to ponder just a few of the things you already know about God, your view of Him would grow higher. For example, think about this: God is present everywhere all the time (omni-present). And everywhere God is He is completely there. Meditate on that—think deeply about it. God is present with you now, fully present. And He always is. There is never less of Him present with you. He is ALL there.

How do you respond to His full-time, full-power, and full-attention presence? Do you delight in it? Are you comforted by it? Afraid? Ashamed? Hopeful? All of these are understandable responses. They reflect on our behavior and circumstances, as well as how we think God responds to what He sees and knows about us. We are comforted by His presence when we are afraid. We are grateful for His presence when we are making difficult decisions. We are ashamed in His presence when we are rebelling.

But let's take the focus off ourselves and meditate on God's presence proactively rather than reactively. Let's set our minds clearly on God and the reality of His constant presence, acknowledging Him many times throughout the day, regardless of what is going on. (This is what believers in past generations called "practicing the presence of God." A practice we would do well to copy.) Wouldn't we be wiser and our faith stronger if we maintained an awareness of God's presence in this way? Think of the difference it would make if you went through each day consciously aware that God is with you, participating in every conversation, protecting you from evil influences, and guiding your thoughts.

Everywhere. All there. All the time. He is God.

Holy dread of displeasing God

This is what many people limit their thoughts to when they hear the term *the fear of the Lord*. It certainly is a part, though not the whole. It is the right response of believers to the sinful desires we still have within us and the sinful things we sometimes do. While we no longer fear the eternal wrath of God's justice, we rightly grieve when we have done something contrary to His will. Whereas we could once sin at will, our hearts are now pulled down when we disobey. We want to please the One we love, the One we respect, the One we desire to honor. Sin has lost a great deal of its appeal and is giving way to a growing love for the Savior who redeemed us from its curse.

Growing hatred of evil

Proverbs 8:13 plainly says, "The fear of the LORD is hatred of evil." It is not just the sin within us that we now despise, but the sin we see all around us. Because we have witnessed the devastation of sin on people, families, and nations, we understand more about its truly evil nature. We are especially repulsed because it caused the suffering and death of Christ.

Why We Must Learn to Fear God

Just as the fear of the Lord sets us on a path of wisdom, not fearing Him leads us toward foolishness and weakness. Here's a pattern I've seen repeated many times:

A Downward Progression

Failure to fear God (not practicing the presence of God) and forgetting who He truly is

Loss of accountability to God (replacing God as the authority in our lives)

Redefining life purpose and commitments without God (practically speaking, we leave God out)

Irresponsible in choices and relationships

Selective obedience and subjective interpretation of Scripture

A life of compromise resulting in a wasted life

When we do not fear God, we lose our respect and awe for who He is, and as a result we do not live our lives as if in the presence of almighty God. As we forget who God is and lose our sense of accountability to Him, we make a play to become our own authority. Then, with God nudged aside, we redefine our purpose and commitments to suit ourselves. This yields a self-serving interpretation of Scripture and selective obedience. If executed over a lifetime, we'll leave the legacy of compromise and a wasted life.

LIFE SKILL: How we learn to fear God

"The fear of the LORD is the beginning of wisdom" (Proverbs 9:10). Psalm 111:10 repeats this and adds, "all those who practice it have a good understanding." Through practicing the fear of the Lord, intentionally calling ourselves to fear Him, we will begin to live wisely. We will be growing in our capacity to do things the way God wants them done.

Consider some of the benefits the fear of God brings:

- The fear of the Lord is riches and honor and life (Proverbs 22:4); it prolongs life (10:27)

- The fear of the Lord is the beginning of knowledge—fools despise wisdom and instruction (Proverbs 1:7)
- The fear of the Lord builds faithfulness (Jeremiah 32:36–40) and keeps us from drifting away from God
- The fear of the Lord brings the fulfillment of our desires (Psalm 145:19)
- The fear of the Lord is a prerequisite for leadership, as seen in the lives of those Moses selected to assist him (Exodus 18:21)
- The fear of the Lord is foundational to relationships (Ephesians 5:21)
- The fear of the Lord brings a clear conscience and a good night's sleep (Proverbs 19:23)
- The fear of the Lord brings God's favor (Psalm 147:11)
- The fear of the Lord protects against danger and evil (Psalm 33:18–19; Proverbs 16:6) and injustice (2 Chronicles 19:5–7)
- The fear of the Lord delivers us from the fear of man (Matthew 10:26–33)

Clearly, the fear of God is not meant to restrict our lives but to direct and fulfill them. Consider, then, what we need to do to reorient our lives around the God who is worthy of our respect.

1. Pray, asking God to teach you to fear Him. (Be aware: He has a lot of methods at His disposal and He is an excellent teacher!)

   Solomon, the wisest man in the world, provides counsel for us in Scripture, which should always be our starting point if we want to know God:

   My son, if you will receive my words and treasure my commandments within you, make your ear attentive to wisdom, incline your heart to understanding; for if you cry for discernment, lift your voice for understanding; if you seek her as silver and search for her as for hidden treasures; then you will discern the fear of the LORD and discover the knowledge of God.

   Proverbs 2:1–5 NASB

2. See God's authority displayed through His judgment of sin.

   There are few scenes in Scripture that are as chilling as the one described near the end of the book of Revelation:

Then I saw a great white throne and Him who sat
upon it, from whose presence earth and heaven fled
away, and no place was found for them. And I saw
the dead, the great and the small, standing before the
throne, and books were opened; and another book
was opened, which is the book of life; and the dead
were judged from the things which were written in
the books, according to their deeds. And the sea gave
up the dead which were in it, and death and Hades
gave up the dead which were in them; and they were
judged, every one of them according to their deeds.
Then death and Hades were thrown into the lake of
fire. This is the second death, the lake of fire. And if
anyone's name was not found written in the book of
life, he was thrown into the lake of fire.

20:11–15 NASB

3. Study biblical characters and their transforma-
   tional encounters with God.

   Here's a starter list:

   • Noah believed God's warning and obeyed by
     building an ark (Hebrews 11:7)

   • Moses received the Ten Commandments (Exo-
     dus 34)

   • David confessed his sin and prayed for a clean
     heart (Psalm 51)

- Jonah's disobedience led to his being cast into the sea, where he was swallowed by a great fish (Jonah 1:13–17)
- Isaiah was transformed by a vision of the holiness of God (Isaiah 6:1–7)
- Saul became Paul when he encountered God and became His messenger (Acts 9)
- John was in awe as he prophesied of the honor and glory that God will receive (Revelation 4:1–11; 5:11–13)

4. Read the stories of those who spent their life seeking God and learning to fear Him.

   The writings and stories of faith will inspire your faith and experience with God. Again, here is a starter list:
   - *The Pursuit of God*, A.W. Tozer
   - *Knowing God*, J. I. Packer
   - *The Knowledge of the Holy*, A.W. Tozer
   - *Through Gates of Splendor*, Elisabeth Elliot
   - *God's Smuggler*, Brother Andrew
   - *The Hiding Place*, Corrie ten Boom
   - *Your God Is Too Small*, J. B. Phillips
   - *The Reason for God*, Timothy Keller
   - *Loving God*, Charles Colson

As I said, practicing the presence of God is crucial to learning to fear Him. This is not some esoteric, impractical mind exercise. It plays into every minute of every day and provides an escape route when temptation leaps into our path. It has done this for me many times. For example:

I was attending the Billy Graham School of Writers Conference in Minneapolis. As I stood before the elevator, waiting as it crept its way to my floor, I gave up and headed for the stairs. Opening the door, I was shocked to see a porn centerfold spread out on the floor of the landing. As I stepped over it, I was amazed at how many thoughts could jet through my mind in the time it took me to take just one step. *Wow! Who would know if I picked it up and stuffed it into my backpack? God will know! I'll end up having to confess it to Barbara too. God will know. God will know. God will know.*

The fear of God turned me away from evil. It does this for us. And so much more.

> "Men who fear God face life fearlessly. Men who do not fear God end up fearing everything."
>
> —Senate Chaplain Richard Halverson

3

Love God, Not the World

Do not love the world or the things in the world.
If anyone loves the world, the love of the Father
is not in him. For all that is in the world—the
desires of the flesh and the desires of the eyes
and pride of life—is not from the Father but is
from the world. And the world is passing away
along with its desires, but whoever does the will
of God abides forever.

—1 John 2:15–17

Life is an arduous journey; God and the world are
competing for your affections. This conflict raises an
important question: Which one do you love most?

If We Love a Person

J. C. Ryle was one of the most influential Christian voices of the nineteenth century. He was an Anglican bishop in England, a straight-shooting gospel preacher who taught thousands how to live a truly holy life. Ryle urges us to think carefully about the nature of love through one of his writings that mirrors the affections between a man and a woman with those we may hold toward Christ. I've abbreviated his list here, adding a few of my own observations.

"If we love a person, we like to think about him (or her)."

If you have ever been in love, you know that your thoughts are drawn to that person. This is the gravitational pull of a love relationship.

"If we love a person, we like to hear about him."

We find happiness in hearing others say good things about the one we love.

"If we love a person, we like to hear from him and read what he has to say."

Nothing brightens our day more than receiving a message from the one who has our heart.

"If we love a person, we like to please him."

We are glad to consult his tastes and opinions, to act upon his advice, and do the extra things that express how much his happiness means to us.

"If we love a person, we like his friends."

We gladly make the effort to become friends with his friends. Our relational circle grows because of the new ties we form through our love.

"If we love a person, we are jealous about his name and honor."

We do not like to hear him spoken against, and we will defend his reputation if others make demeaning remarks or false accusations.

"If we love a person, we like to talk to him."

We tell him all our thoughts, and open up to him about our fears and dreams. We want his counsel, understanding, and reassurance.

"Finally, if we love a person, we like to be always with him."

Thinking, hearing, reading, and talking are each wonderful in their own way. But when we really love a person, we want something more. We long to always be in their company.

As you reflect on these eight descriptions of love, ask yourself: Do these describe my love for Christ? Do I love Him wholeheartedly?

The Greatest Affection

When Jesus was asked which commandment was the greatest, He responded with what could be considered a one-word answer: love.

> You shall love the Lord your God with all your heart and with all your soul and with all your mind. This is the great and first commandment. And a second is like it: You shall love your neighbor as yourself. On these two commandments depend all the Law and the Prophets.
>
> Matthew 22:37–40

God made us for a relationship—with himself and with others. Christ acknowledged both "loves" in His answer, but we must be careful not to overlook the prioritized order. There is a first love, and it is God. Always and only God. If we don't love God supremely, then the world will seduce us with its lure of lesser affections. This is why God warns us, "Do not love the world or the things in the world. If anyone loves the world, the love of the Father is not in him" (1 John 2:15). He knows that in our yearning to love and be loved, our affections sometimes go rogue.

The apostle John goes on to unpack for us the ways we are lured away from God by the world (v. 16). The Scriptures warn of the most seductive forces in the universe, "The Temptation Triplets," competing for the affections of our hearts:

1. *Pleasure*—"the lust of the flesh" (NASB). Pleasure yields an empty life. Solomon tried it: "I said in my heart, 'Come now, I will test you with pleasure; enjoy yourself,'" but concluded, "Behold, this also was vanity" (Ecclesiastes 2:1). Given his wealth and position, few pleasures would have been unavailable to Solomon, but he found them all futile. None were worth the effort he put into them.

2. *Possessions*—"the lust of the eyes" (NASB). Again, we can learn from the trial-and-error approach that Solomon took. In this case, the trial: "And whatever my eyes desired I did not keep from them" (Ecclesiastes 2:10), and the error: "Never satisfied are the eyes of man" (Proverbs 27:20).

If possessions are our love, we will never get all that we want.

3. *Power*—"the boastful pride of life" (NASB). Pride comes down to our efforts to wrest the control of life away from God. We want to call our own shots and have God approve them by blessing us. This pattern can be traced to the beginning of humanity, when the serpent appealed to this way of thinking by asking, "Has God said?" There can be no experience of God's love until we abdicate the throne and confess, "You alone are God!"

We all have our weaknesses. Which of the three is yours?

Many things will compete for first-love status in your life, and each one will be rooted in the pursuit of pleasure, possessions, or power. The best prevention against them, the surest way to keep your heart from being overgrown with lesser affections, is to "love the Lord your God with all your heart and with all your soul and with all your mind" (Matthew 22:37). How you respond to His claims on your life will determine the quality of your life, your destiny, and your legacy.

The Contract and the Gift

Loving God—with *all*—requires surrender. This thought made such an impression on us that Barbara and I made it the focus of the first Christmas we celebrated together as a married couple.

It was December 19, 1972. We were living in a sparsely appointed house in Boulder, Colorado. We had just moved in. We had a borrowed couch, and a cardboard box served as our coffee table. Our dining table was a prize we'd snagged at a local auction. Our Christmas tree, a three-foot Norfolk pine, stood in a corner of our cozy living room (*cozy* is newlywed speak for being long on love and short on cash). We'd decorated the tree with a dozen red ornaments, and placed our presents underneath. There were just a few, so we scattered them out to give the appearance of a bigger haul.

We had decided to mark our first shared Christmas with the most expensive present either of us had to give. As singles we'd heard the president and founder of Cru, Dr. Bill Bright, tell the story of how he and his wife, Vonette, had signed a contract that gave God the "Title" to their lives. So before giving each other our gifts, Barbara and I first wanted to present to God the most valued gift we possessed. Each of us, on our own, spent some time writing out our version of the "Title Deeds to Our Lives."

We listed what we already possessed and all that we desired—the things we thought were important—and said we wanted to give them to Him. This kind of bare-the-soul honesty wasn't easy. Our lists were going to reveal our values and desires, and then we would be yielding everything on those lists to Jesus Christ. He had bought us and redeemed us with His life and death; it was the very least we could give Him. This wasn't an empty religious ceremony—we meant it. Once we finished, we shared our lists with each other, and then signed and dated them. It was a somber moment. We then folded our lists and placed them in an envelope and sealed it. On the outside of the envelope we wrote, "To God Our Father." We then prayed together, saying to God what we'd each processed privately in our hearts.

We kept the sealed envelope in a safe deposit box with our other important papers for eighteen years. I've often said that it was the most important set of papers in there. Then, on an extended vacation in northern Minnesota, with all six of our children present, we opened the envelope. Reading our lists with nearly two decades of life behind us brought both perspective and amusement. We could see the shallowness of some of the things we once deemed valuable, and were embarrassed to think how difficult it had been back then to give those things over to God. For example, my list included:

- Plenty of money (hey, we didn't have a lot; we only made $560/month)
- Nice big house with a workshop and office (I have no idea why I wanted a workshop. I'm not handy!)
- To ski well (we lived in Boulder, Colorado)
- Security
- New car
- A healthy big family—several boys (notice the priority order—doesn't speak well for the guy who ended up giving leadership to FamilyLife!)
- Easygoing job
- Sharp clothes (very spiritual, huh?)

Other things weren't quite so shallow:

- Success in ministry
- To stay healthy
- Barbara
- My own life

Barbara's list was only eight things:

- A house—fireplace, three to four bedrooms, big, pretty two-story with shutters, lots of yard space, yellow frame, bay window
- Children—at least one boy and one girl, who will grow up to glorify God
- To live to see my children grow up
- To have nice clothes and beautiful things and to be an outstanding couple and family
- To develop and be good at skating and watercolor and even skiing (to be talented)
- To be settled and stable
- To always be pretty and attractive
- Dennis

Looking at the list nearly twenty years later, several things hit me. First, even though our contract had been a means of documenting that we were turning away from the world and turning to Christ, my list revealed I had been preoccupied with material things. Second, I had given God very little compared to what He had given me. Third, God had weaned both of us from some of our desires for stuff. We'd grown. And fourth,

Barbara and I had surrendered, separately and jointly, to Another. Surrender to Christ has worked! In fact, I don't know how we'd have done it without surrender.

Now, looking back over forty-five years of marriage and seeking to walk together and experience Him, as well as make an impact for Him, Ephesians 3:20–21 comes to mind:

> Now to him who is able to do far more abundantly than all that we ask or think, according to the power at work within us, to him be glory in the church and in Christ Jesus throughout all generations, forever and ever. Amen.

Far more abundantly than I ever imagined. If we can imagine it, He can exceed it.

Why would you waste another day nibbling at crumbs when you can experience a feast with the King? What is keeping you from complete surrender to Jesus Christ? Take a look at what has captured your heart and ask, *Is this thing that I love a better object of my affection than Jesus Christ? Is it worthy of occupying His place in my life?*

Why not craft and sign your own "Title Deed to My Life"?

Order, Please

To me, life in Christ is a process of God weaning us
from loving this world while increasing our capacity and
experience of loving Him. "The essential task of life is
to set your loves in order" (attributed to St. Augustine).
Although we didn't understand it then, it's essentially
what Barbara and I were attempting to do on Christmas 1972. We were saying that because He first loved
us and because we loved and were committed to each
other, we wanted to put God first in our affections by
yielding all our dreams and plans to Him. He was ours
and we were His. All His.

St. Augustine was really just echoing the "great and
first commandment" of Christ (Matthew 22:37–38).
But, after surrender, what does loving God look like?
How does it show itself and how does it grow?

LIFE SKILL: Learning to love God

In his book *Loving God*, Chuck Colson writes about
asking several Christian leaders and mature followers
of Christ to explain how they expressed loving God
with all their heart, soul, and mind. Some gave rote
religious answers about church attendance and such,
while others described it in more emotional terms.

Others, he said, looked at him suspiciously, as if it were a trick question. This led Colson to the conclusion:

> Most of us, as professing Christians, do not really know how to love God. Not only have we not given much thought to what the greatest commandment means to our day-to-day existence, we have not obeyed it. . . . Perhaps the reason the church was so ineffective in the world was that it had the same needs I did.[1]

Colson's conclusion set me off on another biblical expedition. Since Christ commanded us to love God, certainly He modeled it and taught us how to do it. My search for what He did unearthed four findings.

First, Christ modeled what loving God is by living a life of total surrender to His Father. The Lord's Prayer states it simply: "Thy will be done, on earth as it is in heaven." Christ stated, "Not my will, but Thy will be done" and ultimately demonstrated it by submitting to the Father's plan and going to the cross to die. Ongoing surrender to His heavenly Father was Christ's life. He spoke no words other than the words His Father told Him to speak. He did nothing other than what the Father had for Him to do. Loving God means surrendering to God.

Second, Christ instructs us,

> Whoever has my commandments and keeps them, he it is who loves me. And he who loves me will be loved by my Father, and I will love him and manifest myself to him.
>
> John 14:21

It has been said that the doors of opportunity swing on the hinges of obedience. When we obey God we have the opportunity to know and experience God because of His promise that He will "manifest himself" to us.

Has God ever manifested himself to you because you obeyed Him? That is, has He ever given you a deeper understanding and enjoyment of His nature after you have obeyed Him in some particular way? Perhaps you forgave someone who'd hurt you and you experienced God's pleasure and peace for having done what He wanted you to do. He promises to reveal more of himself as we obey.

Third, Christ gives us a practical way of demonstrating our love for God by giving us a clear command, one that He states twice: "Love one another" (John 15:12, 17). First John 4:19–21 gives the same command while also making it clear that our ability to love others comes only because God loves us:

> We love because he first loved us. If anyone says, "I love God," and hates his brother, he is a liar; for he who does not love his brother whom he has seen cannot love God whom he has not seen. And this commandment we have from him: whoever loves God must also love his brother.

It has been my experience that God keeps a few people in my life that aren't necessarily easy to love, yet I am still commanded to love them. If I say I love God but refuse to love my brother, yes, even the brother who irritates me, God calls me a liar.

And fourth, in saying in essence to Peter, "If you love me, you'll *tend* and *shepherd* my lambs and sheep" (John 21:15–17 NASB), Christ showed the responsibilities of love. If we love God supremely, we are caring for His lambs and sheep; we will be about His mission of telling others about Him, of seeking the lost, and tending to their growth in Christ.

Does your life give evidence that you love God? Are you:

- Surrendered to Him?
- Obeying Him?
- Loving others as you should?
- Joining Him in His mission?

Just saying we love Him is not enough. The journey of a lifetime and the life that really matters begins when you set your loves in order.

4

Believe God, Not the Deceiver

On the last day of the feast, the great day, Jesus stood up and cried out, "If anyone thirsts, let him come to me and drink. Whoever believes in me, as the Scripture has said, 'Out of his heart will flow rivers of living water.'" . . . Jesus said to them, "If God were your Father, you would love me, for I came from God and I am here. . . . You are of your father the devil, and your will is to do your father's desires. He was a murderer from the beginning, and does not stand in the truth, because there is no truth in him. When he lies, he speaks out of his own character, for he is a liar and the father of lies.

—John 7:37–38; 8:42, 44

A man was browsing through the Sears & Roebuck catalog—it was 1938, so people still did such things—looking for items to outfit his office. He wanted his surroundings to showcase his status as an enterprising businessman. A certain item caught his eye, one that seemed perfect for the image he wanted to portray. It was a tastefully mounted brass barometer. Satisfied that he had discovered just the right piece, he ripped the order form from the back of the catalog, filled it out, wrote a check, placed them in an envelope, and walked down to the corner mailbox to send in his order.

The package arrived a few weeks later. Opening the box, he hoped the actual barometer was as spectacular as it had looked in the catalog. He was delighted to find that it was. But his happiness turned quickly to disappointment when he discovered that the barometer was broken; the needle seemed to be stuck in the downward direction, pointing to the section labeled HURRICANE.

Irritated, he repackaged the shipment, being sure to include a note that expressed his frustration along with a demand for a working replacement. Back to the mailbox he went, expecting another several weeks of waiting. However, he found himself walking to the corner just a few days later—to where the mailbox used to be—before the hurricane carried it away.

The barometer had worked after all.

Battleground

We begin our relationship with God by faith (Ephesians 2:8–9), and we are to continue our journey with Him by faith. The apostle Paul tells us,

> Therefore, as you received Christ Jesus the Lord, so walk in him, rooted and built up in him and established in the faith, just as you were taught, abounding in thanksgiving.
>
> Colossians 2:6–7

We live by faith, and we cannot please God without it.

If faith is so basic to our relationship with God, why is it so elusive? Why do we seem to so easily forget God and set aside His plans? Because faith faces a double threat: (1) Our default tendency is to trust ourselves more than God, and (2) our adversary is out to detour our trust in God through doubts, fears, worries, and outright deception (1 Peter 5:8). Our souls are spiritual battlegrounds.

I was reminded of this when Barbara and I were recently in downtown San Diego. We'd enjoyed a delightful dinner and were walking back to our hotel when we turned the corner and saw a transit train painted black. In massive letters was the message: "Coming this fall . . . *THE EXORCIST*." In smaller letters, the chilling tagline read, "Because every soul is a battlefield."

I stood there thinking, *They got that right.*

Too often we casually stroll into the battle unprepared, unaware that our soul is under assault. You see, our adversary is a liar. It is his nature to deceive, to distort the truth, and to convince us to distrust God. Satan loves to insert questions into our thoughts that will lead us to confusion, doubt, and defiance. No matter how strong our faith in God might have been yesterday, Satan is looking for an opening whereby he can get us to doubt God's goodness and move away from Him today.

The first record we have of this diabolical strategy is found in the fifty-seventh verse of the Bible:

> Now the serpent was more crafty than any other beast of the field that the LORD God had made. He said to the woman, "Did God actually say, 'You shall not eat of any tree in the garden'?"
>
> Genesis 3:1

You and I are still reaping the consequences of the doubt Satan stirred up in the hearts of Adam and Eve that day. They questioned not only what God had said but also why He had said it. Satan got them to question both God's authority and also His intent, making their reasoning go something like this: *God can't be completely trustworthy if He has been withholding something from us. He might not even be good.*

Just as God called Adam and Eve to believe Him, He calls you and me to do the same. The Christian who trusts God and submits to Him is a dangerous warrior in the spiritual battle of good versus evil. Beware then, because Satan's strategy has not changed; he is as committed as ever to undermining God's authority and driving a wedge of doubt between you and God. Satan is relentless; he'll fight against you from the inside through doubts and from the outside through the mounting pressures of our decaying culture.

Remember our friend and his barometer? Imagine the difference it could have made had he only believed the truth of the message it tried to tell him. Little did he know what destruction was hiding behind his doubt.

LIFE SKILL: How do we grow in faith?

John 7:37–38 reads,

> On the last day of the feast, the great day, Jesus stood
> up and cried out, "If anyone thirsts, let him come to me
> and drink. Whoever believes in me, as the Scripture has
> said, 'Out of his heart will flow rivers of living water.'"

Is Jesus speaking the truth? Absolutely.

If faith is a requirement in our relationship with
God (it is), and if faith is essential to pleasing God
(again, it is), how do we get it? What can we do to
grow in faith?

Personally, I have found six spiritual disciplines that
will grow your faith "muscle."

1. Be intentional about Bible intake

Faith will not grow without nourishment from
Scripture. If you want a stronger faith, you must get
in the Book and the Book must get in you. Christ makes
this point in John 15, where He uses the imagery of
a branch drawing life-giving nutrients from the vine.
In the same way, He says, we should look to Him and
His word as our life source: "If you abide in me, and
my words abide in you . . ." (v. 7).

The key here is to be intentional. Make the intake of Scripture a central part of your everyday life. Read it, study it, memorize it, talk about it, and listen to sound biblical teaching. But most important, abide in the Vine; make Him the source of your life. If you need some guidance on how to begin, here are a few suggestions.

- Start reading the Bible every day for fifteen to twenty minutes. In that time you could read five chapters from Psalms and one from the book of Proverbs. You would complete both books in a month. Then do it again. The spiritual patriarch and evangelist Billy Graham has used this method for decades.

- Read the first four books of the New Testament, the Gospels of Matthew, Mark, Luke, and John. They tell the story of how Christ lived and what He taught. Immerse yourself in His story.

- Get involved in a study group. Being around those who are serious about studying the Bible and hearing their insights can be invaluable.

- Read a different translation. I really enjoy reading *The Message*, a paraphrase of Scripture by Eugene Peterson.

- I am currently reading and enjoying *The Jesus Story*, a blending of the Gospels by Bill Perkins (Winwick Cambridge, UK: The White Horse Press). It's another look at the life of Jesus in chronological order.

- Join a church that is strong on biblical teaching and makes you think biblically and challenges you to be radical in your faith. You'll get truth, community, and encouragement there—things we all need.

2. Search, discover, write, and take "Vitamin A" daily

Early in my studies at Dallas Theological Seminary, my mentor and friend Dr. Howard Hendricks made a statement that has shaped my life and ministry; he said, "The Christian community today suffers from a 'Vitamin A' deficiency—Application."

I believe that faith grows in direct proportion to (1) a right understanding of God, who He is, and His ways, and (2) how practically you put your faith into action. I call this the Law of Spiritual Maturation. This approach—search, discover, write, and take "Vitamin A," is a combination of the two.

A growing faith demands that you begin a lifetime commitment of search and discovery; you need to be learning more and more about God's nature and His ways. As you make discoveries, begin recording them in a journal so that you can easily access them for review. In essence, I'm challenging you to create a cheat sheet to remind you of who God is and who you aren't.

When I was in college, I used a cheat sheet to study for tests. It wasn't for cheating, of course, but for capturing the essence of what I needed to know. (So, call it an essence sheet if your conscience likes that title better.) The point is, making a habit of recording and reviewing the truth about God will grow your faith.

3. Start a "rock collection"

This particular approach has been especially helpful to me in times of fear, doubt, and confusion. I've found that we all suffer from spiritual amnesia; we all too quickly forget what God has done in the past, and as a result we fail to trust Him in the present. A "rock collection" can do wonders for unbelief.

There is a practice found throughout the Bible of marking significant spiritual breakthroughs with actual memorials—sometimes a celebration, sometimes a song, sometimes a monument, and sometimes all three. People would revisit these memorials when their faith was faint and in need of being restored. For examples, see Joshua 4, 7; Psalm 78, 103, 106:1–25; and Nehemiah 9. You'll notice that some of these mark failures rather than successes, but even those events were (are) worth remembering if they set God's people back on the path of righteousness.

You should begin memorializing the landmarks in your spiritual journey, revisiting them when you need to respond to circumstances with faith. Create these memorials to mark God's answers to big prayers, His provision for a need, evidence of His work in your life and family, His launching you into a new area of ministry, and so on.

If you visit the offices of FamilyLife in Little Rock, you'll find a BIG rock, a two-ton calico limestone rock, standing close to the front entrance. I had it placed there to memorialize God's provision of $11.6 million so that we could move into our building debt free. It is a sizeable reminder to us that God supplies us with what we need in order to do what He has assigned. On it is an engraved message that reads:

Dedicated by Families Who
Wanted to Give God
All the Glory

Start your own "rock collection"—start by recalling the big and little provisions of God in your life. Consider "collecting those stones" by creating a list in your Bible that reminds you of how God provided, and revisit your collection when your faith is faint.

4. Obey

Faith gives birth to obedience and obedience matures faith. There can be no maturity of faith without obedience. Dietrich Bonhoeffer said in *The Cost of Discipleship*: "Only he who believes is obedient; only he who is obedient believes."

The two—obedience and faith—are always found in tandem, each empowering the other.

In his book *Loving God*, Charles Colson explains,

For maturing faith—faith which deepens and grows as we live our Christian life—is not just knowledge, but knowledge acted upon. It is not just belief, but belief lived out—practiced.

It is as simple, and challenging, as that.

5. Read books and mine hearts

Faith is infectious, and if you want to be radical in your faith you will have to go near those who are clearly infected by it.

Go near by immersing yourself in the journey of faith and the stories of men and women who have trusted God in some remarkable circumstances. Read their biographies (see the starter list in chapter 2). Beyond that, you may want to mine the hearts of some of the men and women of faith who are in your church and community, and even your family. Many book-worthy stories will never find their way into a book, so you must go and find them. The stories these saints can tell—stories of God's faithfulness—will slowly infect and affect your faith.

6. Evict unwelcome houseguests

Do not miss this last point—it may be the most important of all. Unbelief has been and remains the Enemy's most strategic ploy from the beginning, asking the question, "Has God said?" The Enemy hates you and has a diabolical plan for your life. He wants unbelief to set up residence in your life.

Look at the evidence from history:

The nation of Israel wandered about in the desert for forty years and perished there because of their unbelief. Read the progression of how they didn't remember God's works, but rebelled, and had "no faith in the promise" (Psalm 106:1–25).

When Jesus walked on the dusty streets of Jerusalem, He applauded great faith but had some of His most searing words for those who lived in unbelief. He marveled at their unbelief and did not do mighty works because of it (Mark 6:6).

I close this chapter with a story and a question.

Of Grasshoppers and Men

As believers we have been called to a life of faith. But here's the kicker: all of our life in Christ—from start to finish—is one long hearing test. Did we hear what God said? Did we believe Him? Did we obey Him? Did we trust Him? Do we believe Him still? Are we obeying Him still? Are we trusting Him still?

Many years ago, while visiting Bill Bright in his office in (what was then) the headquarters of Campus Crusade for Christ in Arrowhead Springs, California, I noticed a small wooden plaque on his desk with this simple inscription: *I'm No Grasshopper.* I immediately recognized where this motto came from—the story of the twelve spies who were sent out by Moses to check out the Promised Land. When the men returned after forty days and gave a report to their waiting comrades, ten of the twelve said,

> We are not able to go up against the people, for they are stronger than we are. . . . all the people that we saw in it are of great height . . . *and we seemed to ourselves like grasshoppers*, and so we seemed to them.
>
> Numbers 13:31–33

But two men of faith, Caleb and Joshua, offered a different assessment: "Let us go up at once and occupy it, for we are well able to overcome it" (v. 30).

Bill Bright did not have a grasshopper mentality; he would have gladly joined the company of Joshua and Caleb that day. Bill Bright was the man whose life of faith challenged me to believe God for too much, not too little.

On the other hand, there are those described in the well-known words of Henry David Thoreau: "The mass of men lead lives of quiet desperation." This could have been said of Joshua and Caleb's weakhearted colleagues, and I wonder if it doesn't also apply to many twenty-first-century Christians in the Western world—people who have settled, gone soft, and gone silent.

Faith doesn't take a census. It doesn't matter if we are joined by many or few. God is the difference maker. Believe Him!

Will you believe God for too much or too little?

5

....

Obey God, Not Your Feelings

Do you not know that in a race all the runners run, but only one receives the prize? So run that you may obtain it. Every athlete exercises self-control in all things. They do it to receive a perishable wreath, but we an imperishable. So I do not run aimlessly; I do not box as one beating the air. But I discipline my body and keep it under control, lest after preaching to others I myself should be disqualified.

—1 Corinthians 9:24–27

Have you ever heard of *Amish forgiveness*? This phrase came to us through great tragedy. Perhaps you remember the story.

In October 2006, a gunman entered an Amish one-room schoolhouse, shooting ten girls, killing five, and then taking his own life. It's a storyline that has become all too familiar to us. A dark-hearted person goes on a killing rampage, taking the lives of those who were where they were supposed to be and doing what they were supposed to do.

Every time it happens, we grieve. The world is a dark and evil place.

This time, however, something unexpected happened, something extraordinary. There was light.

The light came through the men and women of the Amish community—many of them family members of the victims. What did they do that was so unusual? They forgave. They didn't let their loss and their emotions keep them from the courageous obedience that enabled them to forgive in word and in deed.

One of the first members of the community to reach out to the Roberts family—within hours of the shooting—was Henry Stoltzfoos, a board member of the three Amish schools in the area. He was also their neighbor. When Mr. Stoltzfoos came to visit, Chuck Roberts, the shooter's father, was slumped over at the breakfast bar in their home sobbing uncontrollably. As Mr. Stoltzfoos arrived, dressed in his formal visiting attire, he immediately walked over to Chuck, placed his hand on him and said "Roberts, we love you. This was not your doing. You must not blame yourself."[1]

Terri Roberts, the mother of the shooter, said she was amazed by the grace and forgiveness extended to her family by the Amish people of her community, even the parents of the victims. As her neighbors reached out to her, she kept coming back to Ephesians 4:32, "forgiving one another, as God in Christ forgave you."

These men and women chose to ignore their natural inclination in order to respond as they knew God wanted them to. Because of their faith in God, they knew that only forgiveness could heal their families and their community. Retaliation would only make matters worse. Chastising the shooter's family, their neighbors, would solve nothing. Only forgiveness, followed by compassion, could heal and restore. They chose obedience.

Three Misconceptions about Feelings

Far too many of us live on the level of our feelings. Invariably we allow feelings to control our lives. When we feel slighted, we sulk. When we feel wronged, we take revenge. When we feel lonely, we binge. If we fail to check our feelings against the truth of God's Word, they can take up permanent residency. When this happens, our outlook on life becomes distorted and toxic, and we may end up doing things we would never have imagined.

Our feelings mislead us because we don't fully understand them. It is important then, that we identify our misconceptions so that our feelings become subject to truth.

Misconception #1: Faith is just a feeling

My friend, Ney Bailey, wrote a book entitled *Faith Is Not a Feeling*. A survivor of the 1976 Big Thompson Flood in Colorado that took 150 lives, Ney reminds us that no matter how bleak things look, no matter how we feel, we need to believe and obey God's promises and commands. The appearance of things is never the full truth about them. This is why fear so often gets the upper hand, because we believe only what we can see. Don't let your feelings become your identity, or worse yet, the basis of your life, your god.

Misconception #2: Love is just a feeling

Our highly romanticized view of love has weakened its meaning. Marital love fueled only by feelings runs out of gas eventually, sometimes in less than twelve months. In its essence, love is a commitment. It's bedrock obedience to keep your promises, to honor, respect, and give preference to your spouse even when you don't feel like it.

Of course you want romance in your marriage. Who doesn't? And commitment will bring the romance. But romance, as we so often think of it, is such a powerful feeling that it can also destroy marriages. If the feeling is all we're after, we'll go where the feeling is the strongest.

I think this is what happened with many of the Christian leaders we've seen fall morally over the years. Based on the stories I've heard, I'm reasonably certain that the downfall of these men started with small concessions. Their feelings for another slowly overtook their commitment to their spouse and ultimately Christ. In the end, feelings trumped their promise; compromise followed. Failure is usually not a blowout, it's a slow leak.

Had these men and women recognized the dangerous path their feelings were about to take them on, had they known the devastation they would bring to themselves, their families, and to the cause of Christ, they would have extinguished the catalytic chemistry of attraction to another person. They would have turned back before temptation gave birth to sin. They would have obeyed God rather than their feelings (James 1:12–15).

As someone once said, "Sin would have fewer takers if its consequences occurred immediately."

Misconception #3: Forgiveness is just a feeling

Many people are under the false impression that in order to forgive, they must feel like forgiving. However, forgiveness is a choice to obey the commands of Scripture: "Be kind to one another, tenderhearted, forgiving one another, as God in Christ forgave you" (Ephesians 4:32). When we forgive, we choose to give up the right to punish another. We choose to no longer hold on to or rehearse the hurt caused by the offense, and we choose to relinquish any right to retaliate, even if friends try to persuade us to get even.

A number of years ago, I was in a business partnership with a man who wronged me repeatedly. The man had been a good friend, but he took advantage of me. The result: I was faced with not only a sense of profound betrayal but also dissolving a partnership headed for bankruptcy. The wounds were deep and the temptation to get revenge was very real.

God provided three friends, Merle, Al, and Scott, who helped me sell the company. In the end, I was left with more than 150 boxes of records spanning the last ten years of business. Legally, I was told that I could burn each box after its contents reached the ten-year mark. So on January 1 of each year I'd carry the boxes to my fire pit and light them up. This became an annual spiritual health checkup for me: *Had I continued to forgive my business partner, my friend?* It wasn't easy, but I have forgiven him . . . at least ten times!

Faithfulness and Obedience

Obedience to God will demand courage—the courage to say no to self, to feelings, to appetites, to lust—and to say yes to the cross. Our passions must be subordinate to the cross. There will be no Christlikeness without cross carrying and surrender to the gospel of Jesus Christ.

Obedience to God also demands faithfulness—an enduring devotion to Him, your relationship with Him, your calling to serve Him, and even to the suffering He may design or allow for you. By walking with God moment by moment, living in the light of what you know to be right and doing those things that please Him, your life will matter. Each act of obedience will move you in the direction of holiness.

In a previous chapter, I quoted Chuck Colson. He says, "Loving God—really loving Him—means living out His commands no matter what the cost." By "living out" the commands, Colson raises the issue of faithfulness. This means long-term obedience, a lifestyle of obedience, if you will. This is what God wants of us, and it is what's best for us—full time, no breaks, persevering obedience. It's what author Eugene Peterson described through the title of his book *A Long Obedience in the Same Direction*. Hit-and-miss obedience won't cut it. Between the aggressiveness of the devil and the stubbornness of our appetites, our "hits" will come less frequently and our "misses" more. But when we build one act of obedience upon another, upon another, we will be developing a life of faithfulness—a long obedience.

Since I've quoted him and quoted him again, you know that I had great respect for Chuck Colson. Chuck had become a mentor and friend. He had invited me to his home in South Florida in May 2012, but unfortunately (for me) he had a more important appointment with God. So instead of a day of mentoring, I attended his funeral in the Washington Cathedral. To this day, I carry in my Bible the bulletin from his memorial service, which contained Chuck's favorite Scripture and a couple of quotes:

"For to me to live is Christ, and to die is gain."
—Philippians 1:21

"When Christ calls a man, He
bids him come and die."
—Dietrich Bonhoeffer

"Remain at your post and do your duty—for
the glory of God and His Kingdom."
—Chuck Colson

Chuck Colson's conversion and ministry to prisoners was a gift from God to our nation. We need more men and women like him—men and women on His mission.

How Does God Respond to Faithful Obedience?

Whoever has my commandments and keeps them, he it is who loves me. And he who loves me will be loved by my Father, and I will love him and manifest myself to him.

John 14:21

Do you want to know God more? Do you want to experience more of Him? Do you want to have a fuller understanding of God's ways and purposes? Do you want settled peace, stronger faith, and uncorrupted courage? Then you must come to Him through the door of obedience. Daily. Moment by moment. It is a lifetime journey and an adventure of immense proportions and privilege.

Never underestimate the significance of even the smallest act of obedience—or disobedience. Heed the words of C. S. Lewis:

> Good and evil both increase at compound interest. That is why the little decisions you and I make every day are of such infinite importance. The smallest good act today is the capture of a strategic point from which, a few months later, you may be able to go on to victories you never dreamed of. An apparently trivial indulgence in lust or anger today is the loss of a ridge or railway line or bridgehead from which the enemy may launch an attack otherwise impossible.[2]

You have no idea what you're opening yourself up to when you let your appetites have their way. Perhaps it's time to do what's right. Perhaps it's time to obey God.

Forgiveness and Obedience

In 1999 through 2005, FamilyLife hosted a series of arena events called "I Still Do" in cities across the

United States. These were one-day events that uplifted the covenant of marriage and equipped couples to keep their promises for a lifetime. We had as few as 7,000 and as many as 18,000 in attendance in these arenas. There were a lot of surprises at these events, but none bigger than when we called the audience to one small but very significant act of obedience. Let me explain.

I was seated in the front row at the Cincinnati event, listening to one of the speakers address the audience. I had heard the message before, so I must admit that my mind began to wander. My eyes drifted down to the base of the podium, where there was a vase that held a couple dozen vibrant red roses.

As I sat there, I began a conversation with myself about the roses: *They are going to toss those roses in the dumpster at the end of the event. I wonder if there is some way I can take them back home to Barbara.*

Then I thought, *That's selfish. There are 300 volunteers working here today; maybe we should give the roses to some of them.*

Then I was struck with a thought that connected to the whole purpose of the event. *DUH! There are over 10,000 people here in all kinds of struggles in their marriages, and it's likely that at least one of them needs a rose.*

Later, I gave the concluding message of the "I Still Do" event on fulfilling your marriage promise. One of my points was that we must practice both asking for and granting forgiveness in our marriages. I explained that the Scriptures command us to forgive one another as Christ has forgiven us, and that when our spouse comes to us and confesses how he or she was wrong and asks us to forgive them, we have a choice. We can hold on to the hurt, nurse our grudge, and keep on punishing them with silence or with angry words, *or* we can forgive them. And when we forgive another person, it means that we give up the right to punish them.

I then reached down to the vase and pulled out a single rose and began to share with the audience my lapse of attention and my thoughts about taking the roses home to Barbara, then thinking about giving them to volunteers, and finally my conclusion that perhaps someone in this vast audience needed a rose.

I have to tell you as I reached down to get that rose, I felt like what I was about to do was risky. *What if no one comes to get a rose? What if coming to get a rose in front of 10,000 people is just too much?*

But I did it anyway.

I held up the rose and declared it to be a "rose of reconciliation," and asked, "Is there a man or woman in this audience who's been sitting here all day thinking,

'I've wounded my spouse and I need to ask for forgive-ness'? It's not just a way to get a free rose or to ask forgiveness for something trivial that happened on the way to this event. No, you have really hurt your spouse and you want to confess to her or him that you were wrong, that you need to ask for their forgiveness, and you want to say 'I still do.'" Before I got all those words out, I caught movement out of the corner of my right eye. A man who was near the very top of the arena was making his way down dozens of steps, on a mission to get a rose. He was the only person who'd moved. Every eye was on him. He wasn't sprinting, but his feet were moving really fast as he came down those steps and onto the floor, all the way up to the podium, where he tugged a single rose out of the batch of roses. His eyes met mine. I nodded at him.

The massive audience began to applaud as he snagged his rose and began to sprint up the stairs hitting about every third step. The ovation grew. It was a powerful moment for all.

I have no idea what he'd done, but all I know is that when he reached the row where his wife was now standing, they met each other in what seemed like a midair embrace.

After brushing away the tears that had filled my eyes, I looked down at what had been a vase full of roses at my feet. The vase was empty. In a little over sixty seconds, the roses had all been taken.

As I walked out of the arena after the event, I spotted a couple in an embrace . . . her arms wrapped around his neck . . . holding a single rose.

So, at the next event we had vases with more than 200 roses. I made the same offer . . . those were taken in a couple of minutes. Then 400 roses. People flooded out of their seats and formed lines that snaked their way back into the arena. Couples were coming and both were getting a rose, kneeling in front of the podium, exchanging roses and bowing in prayer together.

After watching thousands come forward over the years at events, I became convinced that there are a lot of people who are in need of revisiting some basic commands in Scripture and becoming obedient.

If you are married, I wonder: Do you need to get a rose and give it to your spouse, and ask her/him to forgive you for something specific that you've done that has wounded them?

LIFE SKILL: Learning to obey God

Jesus commanded us to forgive others "seventy times seven," an infinite number of times. Is there anyone you are harboring bitterness toward and need to forgive right now? Is there anyone from whom you need to ask forgiveness right now?

One of the most challenging acts of obedience that you or I will ever encounter is the choice to forgive someone who has deeply hurt us. It can be life changing. This level of obedience, though extremely difficult, is also greatly rewarding. It will affect at least two lives—the forgiver and the forgiven—and probably more.

Perhaps it's not the issue of dealing with bitterness or asking for forgiveness that is your point of obedience today. Whatever it is, I remind you of James 4:17: "So whoever knows the right thing to do and fails to do it, for him it is sin."

Obey God, not your feelings.

6

Worship God, Not Comfort

Though the fig tree should not blossom, nor
fruit be on the vines, the produce of the olive
fail and the fields yield no food, the flock be
cut off from the fold and there be no herd in
the stalls, yet I will rejoice in the LORD; I will
take joy in the God of my salvation. GOD, the
Lord, is my strength; he makes my feet like the
deer's; he makes me tread on my high places.

—Habakkuk 3:17–19

December weather in Arkansas can be fickle. Some
days are more spring than winter, and some are full
winter. This particular day was full winter. Record-
making winter.

Barbara and I were returning from a trip, our flight landing amid the blasts of an Arctic storm. We retrieved our luggage, trudged to our car, removed over a foot of snow from it, and set out for the thirty-five-minute drive home. An hour and a half later, we pulled into the downhill lane that forks into our driveway. Home was in sight. Or it should have been. Instead we saw only darkness. No power.

The inside of the house was only slightly warmer than the outside. So I quickly built a fire in the fireplace, and then embarked on a solo expedition to my shed, where I stored a portable generator. About halfway back to the house, dragging the generator along, I came to the conclusion that the manufacturer and I had different definitions of *portable*.

By one o'clock in the morning, I had strung enough extension cords from the generator to the house to provide some light and run the refrigerator. For the time being, we would have to rely on the fire, blankets, and extra layers of clothing for warmth.

I made one last trip outside to check on the generator. As I approached, I couldn't help but notice that it was making an unfamiliar sound. I got to it just in time to witness a belch of smoke escaping from the motor and then . . . silence. The generator was done. So was I. There was nothing more to do but go to bed. Cold.

Barbara and I spent the next five days trying to stay warm. Our usually toasty home was more like an ice cave, the indoor temperature hovering near forty degrees. I made three trips into town trying to get parts for a portable gas heater that refused to light (all my emergency backup equipment was in full revolt). Finally, I got it repaired and working. Grateful and relieved, I stood over the heater, warming my hands. And that very moment . . . the power came back on.

Within a few hours, our house was habitable again. The heat seemed to transform us. Life was right again, but the challenges weren't over. I now had to confront my love of comfort.

Like most Americans, I've come to expect light with the flip of a switch, heat or cool with the push of a button, and the makings of a meal with the gentle pull of a refrigerator door. I love comfort and convenience. Perhaps too much. I'd learned just how much I loved it by losing it. I had to face the fact that rather than *wanting* comfort I was inching toward *demanding* it.

The problem with comfort is the more of it we have the more of it we want. We'll arrange our lives around being comfortable—which is very much like the lifestyle of idolatry. We'll overspend our days and our dollars in the pursuit of more and more comfort. In the process, we risk functionally dethroning God as He becomes a lower priority and a lesser pursuit.

It's time to sound an alarm. We are sowing the wind and reaping the whirlwind (Hosea 8:7), worshiping that which moves us further from God rather than nearer.

Worship: A Christian Cliché?

We were made to worship God and only God. Blaise Pascal phrased it as a "God-shaped vacuum" in the heart of every man, which can only be filled by God the Creator, made known through Jesus Christ.

I fear that worship has become a cliché, an "insider" term within the Christian community that means less than it ever has. We say we are going to a house of worship, but do we even understand what worship is? We have worship leaders, but many seem to *perform* for the congregation rather than *lead* the congregation. Church services have a "time of worship," but most of us have never been trained and equipped to understand what true worship is and how we are to participate. We attempt worship weekly and weakly.

What is worship, really? It has been defined as "An expression of reverence and adoration for God." The nineteenth-century English writer Thomas Carlyle described it as "transcendent wonder," and William

Temple noted, "Worship is the nourishment of the mind upon God's truth . . . the quickening of the conscience by God's holiness . . . the cleansing of the imagination by God's beauty . . . the response of my life to God's plan."[1] Worship is not something we can delegate to another person or relegate to a certain time. As Christians, a worshiper is who we are and worshiping is what we do.

I've become convinced that we don't do worship very well. It's not something we are naturally gifted to do. We need some training and encouraging when it comes to becoming an effective worshiper.

LIFE SKILL: Learning to worship

How can we become more skillful at worship?

Looking back over the Scriptures—and my life journey—I begin to grasp what the Holy Spirit has been attempting to teach me about worship. It seems He's been dropping bread crumbs to feed and lead me. I haven't arrived, but I have passed several milestones along the way. I'll share the two that have most enriched my relationship with God thus far.

Milestone #1: The truth about God

Jesus' encounter with the woman at the well gives me much hope. She was an outcast, both ethnically and morally. She was a Samaritan, a despised half-breed of mixed Jew and Gentile bloodlines. In the words of one commentator: "a Jewish mongrel." She had morally struck out—divorced five times and now living with a man who was not her husband. To this lowest of the lowly, Jesus initiates a conversation . . . about worship.

> The woman said to him, "Sir, I perceive that you are a prophet. Our fathers worshiped on this mountain, but you say that in Jerusalem is the place where people ought to worship." Jesus said to her, "Woman, believe me, the hour is coming when neither on this mountain nor in Jerusalem will you worship the Father. You worship what you do not know; we worship what we know, for salvation is from the Jews. But the hour is coming, and is now here, when the true worshipers will worship the Father in spirit and truth, for the Father is seeking such people to worship him. God is spirit, and those who worship him must worship in spirit and truth."
>
> John 4:19–24

She's stuck on the issue of location: "Our fathers worshiped on this mountain, but you say that in Jerusalem is the place where people ought to worship." Jesus responds by introducing her to a new way of worship.

Here stands the incarnate God instructing an unlikely candidate in how to worship, explaining to her that worship isn't a place, it's a personal encounter with the Father through Jesus Christ. And she still has no idea who she is talking to. But that is soon to change.

Jesus came to make God known, and in this inspired moment, this eternity-changing encounter, He also explains how to worship. Notice the big idea: God is spirit, and worshiping Him demands that our heart, our spirit, be anchored in truth. There can be no true worship of God without believing the truth about Him. This is why the Bible, the Word of God, is so important to us as believers. The Bible explains the truth about God—His character, His acts, His promises, and what He expects of us.

For example, here are a handful of truths about God that Christ made evident:

He is eternal. He has no beginning and no end.

He is self-existent.

He is the Creator, the Almighty God, the One and Only true God.

He is sovereign.

He is holy, He cannot sin.

He is perfect, complete.

He is love.

He is omniscient, He has all knowledge. He has nothing to learn.

He is omnipotent, He has all power.

He is just.

He is unchanging.

Ponder any one of these statements, and you will find yourself compelled to worship. The truth about God stirs us to adore Him.

Worship is not passive, but active. Worship, then, leads us to act upon the truth we believe.

Milestone #2: The great surrender

The apostle Paul reminded us of a vital aspect of worship when he wrote:

> I appeal to you therefore, brothers, by the mercies of God, to present your bodies as a living sacrifice, holy and acceptable to God, which is your spiritual worship. Do not be conformed to this world, but be transformed by the renewal of your mind, that by testing you may discern what is the will of God, what is good and acceptable and perfect.
>
> Romans 12:1–2

Paul exhorts us to totally surrender ourselves to God. My friend Crawford Loritts points out that the first mention of worship in the Bible involves sacrifice. Abraham had been commanded by God to offer up his son, Isaac. As he was preparing to do what God had commanded, Abraham told his servant, in essence, "The lad and I will go yonder and we will worship and return to you." Abraham was captivated by the preeminence of almighty God. As a result, he trusted God implicitly and obeyed Him completely. And then, seeing Abraham's unquestioning surrender, at the last moment God stopped Abraham from offering his son, supplying a ram as the sacrifice instead (see Genesis 22:1–15).

Sacrifice was at the core of worship in the Old Testament. Offering a sacrifice was central in two of the seven feasts (Passover and Day of Atonement). The people of Israel understood that sacrifices were to be made as a covering for sin and to regain a right standing before God, which then made worship possible.

Actually, sacrifice is still central to worship. In Romans 12, Paul urges us to relinquish all rights to our lives (a living sacrifice) in response to "the mercies of God." These mercies have come to us through Christ who became the sacrifice for all who believe (Hebrews 7:21; 9:12; 10:10). It is the love of God, demonstrated through Christ, that compels us to completely surrender to and utterly worship God.

My encounter with Jesus Christ as a college junior captivated my life. I embarked then on a journey of surrendering my rights and yielding to Him. Christ compelled me then, as He does now, to pick up my cross and follow Him. Full-time surrender. Full-time worship.

The way has not always been easy, but I'm sure it has been far better than the one I would have made for myself. One of my favorite poems, "My Master," describes my journey and encounters with Christ.

> I had walked life's path with an easy tread,
> Had followed where comfort and pleasure
>   led;
> And then by chance in a quiet place,
> I met my Master, face-to-face.
>
> With station and rank and wealth for a goal,
> Much thought for body but none for soul,
> I had entered to win this life's mad race,
> When I met my Master, face-to-face.
>
> I had built my castles and reared them high,
> Till their towers had pierced the blue of the
>   sky.

I had sworn to rule with iron mace,
When I met my Master, face-to-face.

I met Him and knew Him and blushed to see
That His eyes, full of sorrows, were fixed on
   me;
And I faltered and fell at His feet that day,
While my castles vanished and melted away.

Melted and vanished, and in their place
I saw naught else but my Master's face;
And I cried aloud: "O, make me meet
To follow the marks of Thy wounded feet!"

My thought is now for the souls of men.
I have lost my life to find it again,
E'er since alone in that holy place
My Master and I stood face-to-face.
                              —Author unknown

What about you? Are you a partial holdout when
it comes to fully surrendering to Jesus Christ? Maybe
the idea of sacrifice is too scary. My counsel: A wasted
life is even scarier. So give up. Go all in. Sign it over.
It's a true adventure to experience God, life as He has
designed it, and you can begin to practice and experience true worship.

   You won't be sorry.

Power Restored

I like what pastor and author Tim Keller said in a sermon based on Psalm 95:

> Worship is seeing what God is worth and giving him what He's worth. True worship is grasping a truth about God and then allowing that truth to strike you in the center of your being.[2]

True worship is highly relational and deeply responsive to God's goodness and grace toward us. Worship transforms us.

Worship is to our hearts what heat was to my home after a five-day power outage. The house was tolerable during those winter days, but it wasn't vibrant. It wasn't welcoming. It wasn't life-giving. But after the heat was restored, I didn't want to leave.

I've concluded that worship is what we practice and experience as we walk with God on a moment-by-moment basis.

Worship is the result of seeking God and finding Him.

Worship is the result of fearing God and being in awe of Him.

Worship is the result of loving God and knowing Him.

Worship is the result of obeying God and understanding more of His ways.

Worship is the result of believing God and knowing you've pleased Him.

Worship is the result of serving God and making Him known to others.

> "When a man stops believing in God, he doesn't then believe in nothing, he believes anything."
>
> —Attributed to G. K. Chesterton

7

Serve God, Not Self

And I heard the voice of the Lord saying, "Whom shall I send, and who will go for us?" Then I said, "Here I am! Send me."

—Isaiah 6:8

Among the first words written of the early life of Jesus were about His mission and why He came. When God appeared to Joseph, he comforted him and explained what was happening: "Do not fear to take Mary as your wife, for that which is conceived in her is from the Holy Spirit. She will bear a son, and you shall call his name Jesus, for he will save his people from their sins" (Matthew 1:20–21).

Among the last words that Jesus spoke were about the mission He gave to us:

> Go therefore and make disciples of all nations, baptizing them in the name of the Father and of the Son and of the Holy Spirit, teaching them to observe all that I have commanded you. And behold, I am with you always, to the end of the age.
>
> Matthew 28:19–20

This is the Great Commission, the greatest mission a human being could possibly engage in.

It was the summer of 1970. The Jesus Movement had erupted, and looking back, I guess you'd have to say Barbara and I were a part of it.

In the late '60s both of us had encountered the incomparable Christ. His message of love and forgiveness for all people burned in our hearts. The two of us, along with another friend, formed a group on campus at the University of Arkansas called "Radicals for Christ." We published underground Christian newspapers and were on the team that brought Josh McDowell to speak on campus about the person of Jesus Christ. During student elections, we even ran "Christ for Student Body President and Resident of Your Life," publishing a campaign brochure that had the claims of Christ and His offer of forgiveness of sins to all who believe.

We, along with hundreds of others, were on a mission to make Jesus Christ THE issue on campus.

Upon graduation, there was no other cause that came anywhere close to the cause of Christ and making Him known. Barbara and I weren't married at the time. When we graduated, I decided to go to work with Cru (then Campus Crusade for Christ) and share Christ with high school students in Dallas, Texas. Barbara also went to work with Cru, on the University of South Carolina campus.

Each of us, independent of the other, shocked our parents when we informed them we were going to be missionaries on high school and college campuses with Cru, and that we would be raising our personal financial support—to be paid $285 a month.

We were captivated by Christ—who He is, what He taught, His claims on our lives, and how He met the spiritual needs of students' souls. When we were challenged to raise our own support and live a sacrificial lifestyle, it was only logical to give our lives fully to His call. As one man said,

If Jesus isn't who He claimed to be, then all the good that will be done in His name will still be done and it really doesn't matter if we sacrifice. But if He is who He claimed to be, the God-Man, the Son of God, the Savior who died for our sins and offers forgiveness, then nothing else matters.

—Author unknown

Barbara and I were all in. Nearly five decades later, we still are.

About six years later, Barbara and I, as a married couple, would join two other couples and address a need we'd both seen in the lives of college and high school students—the breakdown of the family. Now, having given most of our adult lives to making Christ known in marriages, families, and through orphan care, we have absolutely no regrets. We still raise our own financial support, and if we had it to do all over again, we would. Zero regrets.

The Self-Serve, "Have It Your Way" Society

How about you? Any regrets?

It's difficult not to want to have it all, and to have it your way. You and I are daily confronted with advertisements that tell us that what we have is not enough. We deserve more, and we deserve it now. Infinite entertainment options, on demand, on a mobile device or computer. A new car, on credit. A bigger house. All this caused pastor and author Rick Warren to quip that many people are driven by "aimless distraction."

In this culture, no one is exempt from the lure of lesser loyalties. They compete for the affection and allegiance of our souls.

I'm reminded of what C. S. Lewis said in his book *The Great Divorce*: "There are two kinds of people: those to who say to God, 'Thy will be done,' and those to whom God says, 'All right, have it your way'" (my paraphrase).

Finding Purpose

Contrast a life lived serving self with one lived serving God—one who purposed to live for another: King David. Here was a man whose legacy was checkered with all kinds of compromises and failures—lies and deceit, adultery, murder, and a final bitter rant on his deathbed. Surely his obituary would not read well. But tucked away in the book of Acts is an incredible summary of David's life: "For David, after he had served the purpose of God in his own generation, fell asleep and was laid with his fathers" (Acts 13:36).

Two observations:

1. Despite his many failures, he repented and sought God.
2. Despite his many failures, he served the purpose of God.

So, what have you done that disqualifies you from being used by God? Answer: If you have repented, NOTHING. We all make excuses for why we think God can't use us:

- I've made mistakes, God can't use me.
- I still sin, God won't use me.
- I'm out of step with God. (Then get in step!)
- I'm not useable. (Then become useable.)
- I'm not gifted enough, eloquent enough, bold enough, or educated enough. (Then read about David, Moses, and others who went from useless to useable.)

Related to the second observation, I ask: Are you engaged in God's purposes for your generation?

Perhaps a better question is: Do you have a purpose? And if you do, what is it? Thomas Carlyle wrote, "A man without a purpose is like a ship without a rudder."

You were not made for just any purpose; you were made for God's purposes. The Scriptures declare it: "For we are his workmanship, created in Christ Jesus for good works, which God prepared beforehand, that we should walk in them" (Ephesians 2:10).

You are not just anyone, a random set of molecules and DNA. You are His "work of art," created by Him on purpose for His purposes. You will never determine your purpose apart from God. Atheist Bertrand Russell ironically declared, "Unless you assume a God, the question of life's purpose is meaningless." Even those who don't profess to follow Christ recognize our need for purpose. Irish playwright and Nobel Peace Prize winner in literature, George Bernard Shaw wrote,

> This is the true joy of life, the being used for a purpose recognized by yourself as a mighty one, the being thoroughly worn out before you are thrown on the scrap heap; the being a force of Nature instead of a feverish selfish little clot of ailments and grievances complaining that the world will not devote itself to making you happy.[1]

So what's your purpose? Who or what is your purpose centered on? God's agenda? His kingdom's work? His message—that He came to seek and to save the lost? What's keeping you from fulfilling His purposes in your generation?

There comes into the life of every person a task for which he or she alone is uniquely suited. What a shame if that moment finds us either unwilling or unprepared for that which could become what Churchill referred to as "our finest hour."

LIFE SKILL: Learning to serve on purpose

In giving leadership to FamilyLife and building a team of several hundred staff over the past forty years, it might surprise you that I've actually done more career counseling than marriage and family counseling. I have found a growing number of people who want to live their lives fully engaged in serving God's purposes. Here are the main issues I encourage each one to consider.

Debunk the ministry myth

You don't have to draw your paycheck from a church or mission organization to be in ministry. This misconception has caused many people to miss serving where God already had them planted. You don't have to be a seminary graduate to be used by God. It may be that where you are already gives you very strategic influence and impact for God's purposes.

Seek God

If God made you, and He did, then He is where you must start. Surrender your life to Him, if you haven't yet. I'm not a gambler, but I like the term *Go all in.* Don't hedge your bets. The more you connect with God, the more confident you'll become that you are where you need to be, doing what He has designed you to do.

Look for "passion prints" in the past

Ask God to help you inventory your passions. What do you pound the table about? What need do you see that is truly worth giving your whole life to?

Like tracking footprints in the snow, look back over your life and look for "passion prints." Look for how you have engaged in something and sensed the pleasure of God. Many times it is the affirmation of others that confirms that God is using you; they recognize it more objectively than you do.

Check your hard wiring

What is effortless for you? Second nature? What is it you love doing? If it is true that "you are His work-manship" for good works, then I promise you He knew what He was doing when He made you. God doesn't make mistakes. And He even delights in using your mistakes for His purposes.

Are you more of a task person or people person? Are you a behind-the-scenes deliverer or are you gifted to be up front? Are you a teacher? Encourager? A starter of things? A finisher of things? A project person or a creative person? Manager or entrepreneur?

Embrace your identity

Second Corinthians 5:20 clearly states that you are an ambassador. This means that your home is an embassy, representing the King and His kingdom. If you are going to engage in a spiritual enterprise (and battle), you must know *whose* you are and *who* you are. You are His "agent," commissioned to be engaged in His global agenda.

A Snail's Pace

Faithfulness is the currency of kingdom work. Serving God will involve perseverance. There are no perfect jobs on this side of heaven. Expect thorns and thistles to crop up, often disguised as people. You and I must learn to persevere.

You know by now my love of meaningful quotes, the ability God has given some people to load their words with truth. Here is one I turn to often, and one which Charles Spurgeon often referred to: "It was by perseverance the snail reached the ark."

A close second are these rather chilling words from George W. Cecil, under the pseudonym William A. Lawrence: "On the 'Plains of Hesitation' bleach the bones of countless millions, who at the very dawn of victory, sat down to rest, and while resting, died."

In other words, Don't quit!

Christ Alone

Christ has staked a claim on your life. Be glad of it. He is incomparable. It is your calling, and your honor, to serve Him. There is no other way to live a life that matters.

Jesus Christ didn't come to take sides; He came to take over.

Jesus Christ didn't come to be a spare tire; He came to be the driver.

Jesus Christ didn't come to get your attention for a couple of hours a week; He came to be the center of your existence.

Jesus Christ didn't come for your leftovers; He came to be lavishly loved, wholeheartedly.

Jesus Christ didn't come just for your hands and feet; He came for your heart—all of you.

Jesus Christ didn't come only to save you from God's future wrath; He came to be your Redeemer, Lord, and life-giver today.

Jesus Christ didn't come just to be your friend and confidant; He came to be obeyed, trusted, and worshiped.

Jesus Christ didn't come to make you comfortable; He came to make you secure and to enlist you in His exhilarating mission.

Jesus Christ didn't come to give you a good life; He came to give you His life.

Jesus Christ will not come back as a Lamb; He will return as the conquering King of kings, Lord of lords, the Lord God Almighty!

> "God is looking for people through whom He can do the impossible; what a pity we plan to do the things we can only do by ourselves."
>
> —A.W. Tozer

Epilogue

To seek God is the greatest quest.

To fear God is the greatest respect.

To love God is the greatest affection.

To obey God is the greatest act.

To believe God is the greatest adventure.

To worship God is the greatest experience.

To serve God is the greatest privilege.

All this so that God may be glorified and exalted.

I conclude with two great reminders of who this God really is:

> Therefore God has highly exalted him
>
> and bestowed on him the name that is above every name,
>
> so that at the name of Jesus every knee should bow,
>
> in heaven
>
> and on earth
>
> and under the earth,
>
> and every tongue confess
>
> that Jesus Christ is Lord, to the glory of God the Father.
>
> —Philippians 2:9–11

One Solitary Life

Here is a man who was born in an obscure village, the child of a peasant woman. He grew up in another village. He worked in a carpenter shop until He was thirty. Then for three years He was an itinerant preacher.

He never owned a home. He never wrote a book. He never held an office. He never had a family. He never went to college. He never put His foot inside a big city. He never traveled two hundred miles from the place He was born. He never did one of the things that usually accompany greatness. He had no credentials but himself. . . .

While still a young man, the tide of popular opinion turned against Him. His friends ran away. One of them denied Him. He was turned over to His enemies. He went through the mockery of a trial. He was nailed upon a cross between two thieves. While He was dying His executioners gambled for the only piece of property He had on earth—His coat. When He was dead, He was laid in a borrowed grave through the pity of a friend.

Nineteen long centuries have come and gone, and today He is a centerpiece of the human race and leader of the column of progress.

I am far within the mark when I say that all the armies that ever marched, all the navies that were ever built; all the parliaments that ever sat and all the kings that ever reigned, put together, have not affected the life of man upon this earth as powerfully as has that one solitary life.[1]

Choose a life that matters!

Notes

Chapter 2: Fear God, Not Men

1. From the preface of A.W. Tozer, *The Knowledge of the Holy* (Glendale, CA: Bibliotech Press edition, 2016).

2. A.W. Tozer, *The Pursuit of God* (Mockingbird Classics edition, 2016).

3. Wilbur E. Rees, *$3.00 Worth of God* (King of Prussia, PA: Judson Press, 1971), 104–105.

4. Patrick Morley, *The Man in the Mirror* (Grand Rapids, MI: Zondervan, 1989).

Chapter 3: Love God, Not the World

1. Charles Colson, *Loving God* (Grand Rapids, MI: Zondervan, 1987).

Chapter 5: Obey God, Not Your Feelings

1. Adapted from Terri Roberts and Jeanette Windle, *Forgiven* (Minneapolis, MN: Bethany House, 2015).

2. C. S. Lewis, *Mere Christianity* (HarperCollins).

Chapter 6: Worship God, Not Comfort

1. *Readings in St. John's Gospel* (Compiled from the Gifford Lectures, Glasgow, between 1932–1934 by Temple). First published in two volumes in 1939, 1940, Macmillan & Company, St. Martin Press.

2. In a sermon titled "The Freedom of the Truth," given by Timothy J. Keller at Redeemer Presbyterian Church, May 8, 1994.

Chapter 7: Serve God, Not Self

1. George Bernard Shaw, *Man and Superman*, Epistle Dedicatory to Arthur Bingham Walkley (1903), 29.

Epilogue

1. This essay was adapted from a sermon by Dr. James Allan Francis, titled "Arise, Sir Knight!" in *The Real Jesus and Other Sermons* (Philadelphia: Judson Press, 1926), 123–124.

Dennis Rainey is president and cofounder of Family-Life, a ministry of Cru. He is a graduate of Dallas Theological Seminary and hosts conferences on marriage, men's ministry, and parenting. Dennis is the senior editor of the HOMEBUILDERS COUPLES SERIES and the daily host of the nationally syndicated radio program *FamilyLife Today*. He and his wife, Barbara, live in Little Rock, Arkansas. Their six adult children are all married and have made their parents proud with twenty-three grandchildren.

For more information about
Weekend to Remember marriage getaways
FamilyLife Today
Other resources
go to
Familylife.com
Familylife today.com
or
call 1-800-FLTODAY